# John Clark

## Consulting Editor: Richard Hantula

GARETH**STEVENS**
PUBLISHING
A Member of the WRC Media Family of Companies

Please visit our web site at: www.garethstevens.com
For a free color catalog describing Gareth Stevens Publishing's
list of high-quality books and multimedia programs,
call 1-800-542-2595 (USA) or 1-800-387-3178 (Canada).
Gareth Stevens Publishing's fax: (414) 332-3567.

Library of Congress Cataloging-in-Publication Data

Clark, John.
    Light and sound / John Clark. — North American ed.
        p. cm. — (Real world science)
    Includes index.
    ISBN 0-8368-6306-2 (lib. bdg.)
    1. Light—Experiments—Juvenile literature.   2.  Sound—Experiments—
Juvenile literature.   I. Title.  II. Series.
    QC360.C56   2006
    535—dc22                                                    2005054152

This North American edition first published in 2006 by
**Gareth Stevens Publishing**
A Member of the WRC Media Family of Companies
330 West Olive Street, Suite 100
Milwaukee, WI  53212  USA

Project Editor: Kate Latham
Editor: Anna Claybourne
Inside design: Rachel Clark
Illustrators: Phil Ford and Peter Bull Studios
Educational Consultant: John Stringer BSc
Gareth Stevens editor: Leifa Butrick
Gareth Stevens art direction: Tammy West
Gareth Stevens cover design: Dave Kowalski
Gareth Stevens production: Jessica Morris & Robert Kraus

Picture credits:  © Corel: cover; Bruce Coleman Collection 12, /Peter Hinchliffe 5; Mary Evans Picture
Library 21; Image Bank 6, 8, 19, 22, 25, 29 Oxford Scientific Photos /Daniel Cox 27, /David Dennis 10,
/Mike Linley 15b; Premaphotos 15t.

Printed in the United States of America

1 2 3 4 5 6 7 8 9 10 09 08 07 06

# Contents

# Let There Be Light!

**Everyone knows about light. It comes from the Sun, from lightbulbs, candles, streetlights, and car headlights, and it surrounds us most of the time. What exactly is it? Light is a type of energy – just like heat, electricity, sound, and movement. Unlike other forms of energy, we can see light. Without it, we can't see a thing!**

## Where's it from?

During the daytime, most of the light around you comes from the Sun. As well as helping you to see, sunlight is good for you. Your body uses it to make vitamin D, which helps make your bones stronger. It also provides warmth, which is particularly useful when you want to dry off on the beach after a swim. Plants need sunlight, too, because they use it to make food. Inside a plant's leaves, water from the soil and carbon dioxide (a type of gas) from the air combine to make the food chemicals the plant needs to grow and be healthy. Energy from sunlight is used to power this chemical reaction, which is called photosynthesis, meaning "making with light."

Of course, it's not always sunny. Sometimes it's dark. (You'll find out why later.) We have to make our own light then, by turning other kinds of energy into light energy. The earliest lamps were candles and oil lamps. They work by burning fuel, such as wax or oil, which contain chemical energy that came originally from the Sun. As a fuel burns, its chemical energy turns into light energy. The fuel also gives off heat energy, which is why candles and lamps are hot to the touch. We still use candles, but nowadays we rely more on electric lights. Inside a lightbulb, electric energy heats a very thin piece of metal until it is white hot and gives off light. The light in a fluorescent tube or a TV screen comes from phosphors – chemicals that glow when energy flows through them.

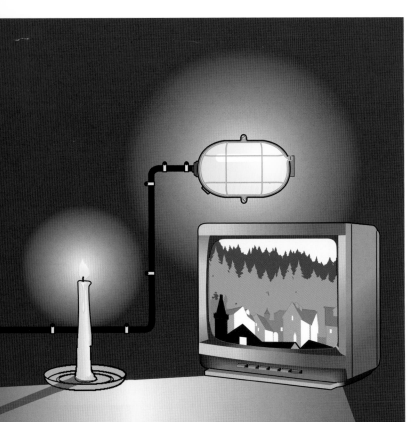

**Candles, light bulbs, and phosphors are all light sources.**

Some watches have hands that glow in the dark. You can also buy glow-in-the-dark stars to stick on your ceiling. How do they work? The answer is luminescence (which simply means "shining"). They contain special chemicals that soak up light during the day and then release it when it's dark. Some animals, including fireflies, glowworms, and some types of fish, are "bioluminescent," which means they can glow in the dark, too. Chemicals in their bodies react with each other to give off light. Unlike most other ways of making light, this does not give off heat energy. This is just as well, or fireflies would cook themselves!

Glowworms attract food by glowing in the dark.

# TRY THIS

## Energy race

This experiment shows that light travels faster than sound. You will need a couple of objects to bang together, such as two pot covers. Ask a friend to stand about 65–100 feet (20–30 meters) from you, facing you. Have your friend bang the two objects together. You will see the action before you hear it. When you see an object, light bounces off it and into your eyes. The light zooms from your friend to you superfast – at the speed of light, in fact. It will be a fraction of a second, however, before you hear the clang. This is because sound travels more slowly than light.

# Amazing Fact

The energy that falls on Earth as sunlight takes up to millions of years to get from the center of the Sun to Earth. The last part of its journey – from the outer parts of the Sun to us – takes just eight and one-half minutes.

# Making Shadows

One of the most important things to know about light is that it travels in straight lines. This is how light makes shadows. Instead of curving around an object, light shines straight past it, making a shadow of the object where the light couldn't get through. This is why your shadow on the ground or a wall is the same shape as you.

## In the shadows

When you're in a shadow, it means there's something between you and a light source, such as the Sun. The biggest example of this is nighttime, which is a kind of giant shadow. At night, your part of Earth is facing away from the Sun. The Sun is still shining, but the light hits the other side of Earth and zooms straight past it, out into space. The side facing away from the Sun is left in darkness.

## Opaque or transparent?

Objects cast shadows because light cannot pass through them. In other words, they are opaque. When light hits an opaque object, it either bounces off or is absorbed (soaked up) into the object. Shiny objects, such as mirrors, make lots of light reflect (bounce) off them. Rough, dark objects, such as a piece of black cloth, absorb most of the light that hits them. Other objects, like your body, reflect some light and absorb the rest. Light that is absorbed turns into heat.

Not all objects are opaque. If they were, our windows and eyeglasses wouldn't be of much use! Transparent substances such as glass and clear plastic let light shine right through them. They don't make a dark shadow. Glass in normal windows, which we can see through, is perfectly flat on both sides, but if one side is roughened or embossed with a pattern, it scatters the light. It still lets light through, but you can't see through it clearly. That's why it's often used for bathroom windows.

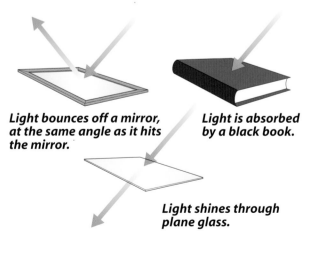

*Light bounces off a mirror, at the same angle as it hits the mirror.*

*Light is absorbed by a black book.*

*Light shines through plane glass.*

In a solar eclipse, the Moon casts its shadow on Earth. Where the Sun is fully hidden is called the umbra of the eclipse. The larger shadow, the penumbra, is where part of the Sun is visible.

# Did You Know?

An eclipse happens when the Sun, the Moon, and Earth line up in space. In a solar eclipse, the Moon moves between Earth and the Sun. The Moon blocks out light from the Sun, making a huge shadow fall across Earth. If you are standing right in the middle of this shadow, you see a total eclipse, and it's almost as dark as nighttime.

# Amazing Fact

If you were standing in a shadow on the planet Mercury, you would be more than 330°F (600°C) colder than if you were standing in direct sunlight. Brrrrr!

# TRY THIS

## Make a sundial

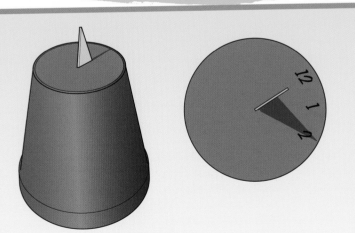

A sundial is one of the oldest ways of telling the time. It uses shadows cast by the Sun. To make a sundial you'll need a right triangle made of stiff cardboard with sides 3 inches (8 centimeters) long, some tape, and a large plant pot. Turn the plant pot upside down and tape the triangle so it stands up on the pot's base. At noon on a sunny day, turn your sundial so that the triangle casts only a thin line of shadow. Use a felt-tip pen to mark this position and label it "12." Leave the pot in the same position, and label the positions of the shadow at 1 o'clock, 2 o'clock, and so on. The following morning (if it's still sunny!) you can mark the positions of the shadows corresponding to the morning hours. Once you've marked all the daylight hours, you can use your sundial as a clock during the day.

# Mirror Images

We see some objects because they give off light, but most things are different. We see them because light bounces off them into our eyes. Some surfaces reflect light better than others. A mirror reflects light completely, and so we see an image of what is directly in front of the mirror. Or do we?

## Seeing is believing

The image in a flat, or plane, mirror is the same size as the reflected object, but reversed left to right. If you look at your reflection and wink your right eye, the reflection winks its left eye. Objects reversed in this way are called – surprise, surprise – mirror images.

The images in curved mirrors are different. A mirror that curves outward is called a convex mirror. It gives a wide view with a small image that is right-side up. The rearview mirror in a car is a convex mirror. A concave mirror curves inward. Distant objects are reflected to give a smaller, upside-down image, but objects that are close to the mirror appear right-side up and bigger. Concave mirrors are used for shaving mirrors. You can see these different reflections if you look at the back (convex) and the inside (concave) of the bowl of a polished metal spoon.

With a plane mirror, the object is the same distance in front of the mirror as the image that appears "behind" the mirror.

## Did You Know?

If you've ever been at a hall of mirrors at a fairground, you'll have seen some pretty strange reflections! They are made using a combination of convex and concave surfaces in the same mirror. The convex parts make you look smaller, while the concave parts make you look bigger. Together, they make you look like something from another planet!

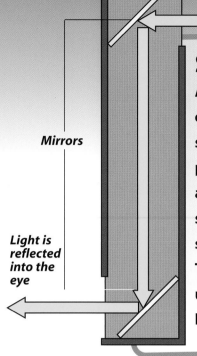

*Mirrors*

*Light is reflected into the eye*

TRY THIS

## See around corners

A periscope uses mirrors to help you see around corners or over walls. Submarines have periscopes so that people inside the submarine can scan the sea surface for danger. To make a simple periscope, you'll need a long, narrow cardboard box (the kind that aluminum foil comes in will do, but make sure it's empty first), two small mirrors, scissors, and tape. Tape the two mirrors in the box as shown here. They must face each other at exactly the same angle. Then tape the box shut and cut out holes opposite each mirror. You use the periscope by looking into one of the holes. The mirrors will let you see out of the other hole.

## Ghostly glass

Plane glass is transparent, but its surface reflects some light, so it can also act as a mirror. You've probably seen your reflection in a store window, for example. By using reflections, a large piece of plane glass can be used to put a ghost on the stage! The audience sees the actors on the stage through a large piece of glass, while a mirror is used to reflect the image of an actor playing a ghost onto the glass. The actor is really underneath the stage, out of sight of the audience.

Amazing Fact

Scientists have measured how far it is to the Moon by reflecting light from a laser off a mirror which was placed on the Moon by astronauts. Since they already knew how fast light travels, the time that the light took to bounce back told them the exact distance to the Moon.

TRY THIS

## Making mirrors

Take a piece of new kitchen foil and smooth it carefully. The bright side makes a fairly good mirror. Nearly all the light that hits the foil is reflected in the same direction, but if you crumple the foil into a ball and then flatten it out again, it makes a very poor mirror. Why? The foil itself has not changed, and it is still reflecting the same amount of light, but the reflective surface now consists of lots of small mirrors at different angles that reflect the light in different directions. Good mirrors have a perfectly flat surface, which is why most of them are made of glass.

# Around the Bend!

Light always travels in straight lines, but it can change direction if it is reflected from a surface. Surprisingly, light also changes direction when it shines through something transparent, such as glass or water. This is called refraction, and it's very useful. It makes lenses in eyeglasses, telescopes, and microscopes work.

## Bent light

When a beam of light passes through a piece of glass or into water, it slows down very slightly. If the light enters at an angle, slowing down makes it change direction, and the beam is bent.

Why does slowing down make the beam bend? In order to understand this, imagine an army of soldiers marching in rows of three. If they march at an angle off smooth ground onto a plowed field, the soldiers who step on the soil first will have to slow down before the others. So for a few steps, one end of the row will go faster than the other, and the group will swing around.

**The straw seems to change size and shape as the reflected light is refracted by the glass and then by both the glass and the colored water.**

## TRY THIS

### Bending light

You'll need a flashlight, a piece of cardboard, scissors, and a glass bottle filled with water along with a few drops of milk. In a dark room, make a beam of light by shining the flashlight through a narrow slit in the piece of cardboard. Shine it through the glass bottle filled with milky water to see how the glass and water bend (refract) and scatter the light.

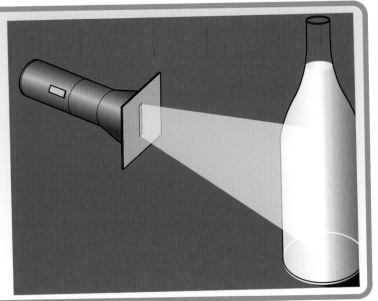

# Lens control

We can control the way light bends by giving the surfaces of a piece of glass a curved shape. A curved piece of glass like this is called a lens (from the Latin word for lentil, because some lenses look like a lentil seed). There are two main kinds. A lens with the surfaces curved outward is called a convex (or converging) lens. Parallel rays of light passing through it are brought together so that they converge to a focus. A magnifying glass is a kind of convex lens. It bends rays of light so that when you look through the glass, objects look bigger. A lens with its surfaces curved inward is a concave lens. It makes parallel light rays move apart or diverge. Objects seen through a concave (or diverging) lens appear smaller than they really are. Both types of lenses are used in eyeglasses, cameras, and optical instruments such as telescopes and microscopes.

**Light enters the eye.**

**Actual insect**

**Magnified image of insect as it appears to your eye from the other side of the lens**

**Lens in a magnifying glass**

**An insect seen through a magnifying glass is magnified as the convex lens bends the light rays.**

Giant objects in space have a strong enough pull of gravity to bend light rays. Stars are sources of both heat and light. The light from stars normally travels in straight lines, but if this light passes close to a galaxy or a group of galaxies, which contain billions of stars, the enormous pull of the galaxy's gravity bends the passing light rays, just as light bends when it travels through a lens. This effect is called a gravitational lens.

The first person to use a microscope to study living things was the Dutchman Anton van Leeuwenhoek (1632–1723). He made his own microscopes. They were simple affairs, with a tiny single convex lens, made by grinding down a bead of glass, but they were powerful enough to see blood cells and bacteria. Modern microscopes have several lenses.

# Rainbow Colors

**Light often appears to be colorless, but sunlight is actually made up of a range of different colors. If that sounds unlikely, think about a rainbow in the sky. Rainbows are made of pure sunlight.**

**Can you see seven colors in this rainbow? You should see red, orange, yellow, green, blue, indigo, and violet.**

## Refracting rainbow

A rainbow is a special example of refraction. You see the colors because when sunlight shines through raindrops, it bends, but the drops of water bend some of the colors that sunlight is made from more than others. This makes the rays of light spread out into the colors of the rainbow.

## Spectrum magic

Around 1665 the English scientist Isaac Newton (1642–1727) made an artificial rainbow by passing a beam of sunlight through a prism (a solid glass shape). The prism bent each color of light a different amount. The result was numerous colored bands, called a spectrum, which followed the colors of a rainbow. Newton recognized the spectrum as being made up of seven main colors: red, orange, yellow, green, blue, indigo (dark blue), and violet (purple).

When light from the Sun is reflected inside raindrops, the drops act like individual prisms and split the light into rainbow colors.

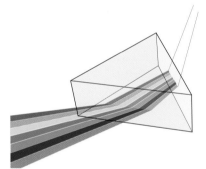

**Light is split into a spectrum of colors by a prism.**

## Seeing red

When "white" sunlight hits an object, it actually shines all the colors of the rainbow on it. Why does a red book look red? What happens is that the book absorbs all of the rainbow colors in sunlight except red. Only red is reflected back to our eyes, and that is the color we see. The same is true for green objects, blue ones, or those of any other color. Black objects absorb all the light rays, so none are reflected back into our eyes, and white objects reflect all the light rays.

## Make a rainbow

You can make your own rainbow or spectrum by using a bowl of water and a small mirror. Fill a bowl or shallow dish with 1 inch or so (2–3 cm) of water. Now hold the mirror at an angle so that the Sun shines on it below the surface of the water. The Sun's rays will be reflected at an angle. Now hold a piece of white paper to "catch" the reflected Sun. Can you see a rainbow? WARNING: do not look directly at the reflection of the Sun in the mirror, because it can damage your eyes.

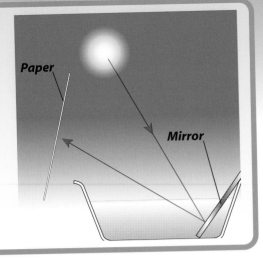

*Paper*

*Mirror*

Color filters let through only one color of light. Any transparent, colored substance can act as a filter. Try looking through colored candy wrappings or one side of a pair of 3–D glasses. If you look at a white cloud through a filter, the cloud takes on the color of the filter. The whole spectrum of colors will be reflected, but the filter will let only the one color through, but if you look at a colored object, such as a green book cover, its color will change depending on the color of your filter. Through a red filter, it will look black because the red won't let the reflected green light through.

## Mixing colors

You know that white light can be split up into the colors of the rainbow. You can also mix the colors to turn them back into white. You will need a circle of white cardboard, about 4 inches (10 cm) across, and a pencil. Divide the card into seven sectors, each stretching from the center to the edge, and color them red, orange, yellow, blue, green, indigo, and violet. Push the pencil through the center of the card and spin it like a top. If you can spin it fast enough, the colors will combine and the circle will look greyish white. (The edges of the card will look whiter than the center because they spin faster than the center.)

Although light has many colors, it is made up of three main, or "primary," colors – red, green, and blue. Any other color of light can be made from a mixture of these three, which is how a television set produces a color picture. The picture that appears on the screen is made up of tiny dots of red, green, and blue light. In different mixtures, these three colors create the shades making up the picture.

# Seeing the Light

Eyes can see things because they "collect" light from objects. Objects either give off their own light or reflect light from another light source. Your eyes detect the light and turn it into nerve messages that go to your brain. Finally, your brain converts the nerve messages into images in your mind. So your sense of sight depends on your eyes and your brain working together.

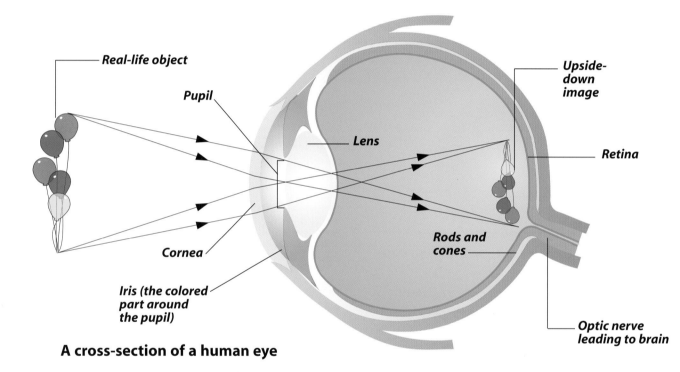

**A cross-section of a human eye**

## Camera eyes

The human eye is constructed like a camera (although eyes came before cameras, so it's really the other way round). Light enters the eye through a window at the front of the eyeball called the cornea. It then passes through the pupil, the black hole at the center of the eye.

The lens inside the eye focuses light rays onto the light-sensitive retina at the back of the eye. Cells called rods and cones cover the retina. These cells trigger nerve impulses when they are struck by light. The nerve impulses pass along the optic nerve to the brain, where they are interpreted as images.

The brain also has another job to do. If you have used a magnifying glass to focus an image on a piece of paper, you know that the image appears on the paper upside-down. So do the images at the back of the eye. Fortunately, our brain turns them right-side up without us having to tell it to do this.

Many insects, such as flies and butterflies, appear to have two eyes, just like humans. Instead of being single lenses like ours, their eyes are made up of thousands of tubes, bundled together like straws. At the end of each tube is a tiny lens. Their eyes are called compound eyes, and they allow insects to see all around them, which is why it is so difficult to catch a fly.

Horseflies use their huge compound eyes to locate juicy, blood-filled animals.

## 3-D vision

Having two eyes a slight distance apart helps give you 3-D vision. Scientists call it stereoscopic vision. Each eye sees a slightly different view, and the brain combines the different images to figure out how far away an object is. Try closing one eye and looking around an unfamiliar room or scene. It's much more difficult to figure out how far away things are with only one eye. Don't even try pouring a glass of water!

## Seeing color

The light-sensing cells called rods, which are mostly around the edge of the retina, detect black, white, and grey. The cones detect color and are in the middle of the retina. In a room with dim lighting, hold up a colored object at the side of a friend's head, while he or she looks forward. Can your friend tell what color it is? Move the object slowly around until it is in front of the eyes. When could your friend see its color?

## Amazing Fact

The human eye can see 10 million different colors, but some creatures can see beyond the rainbow of colors that we see. Snakes that home in on the body warmth of their prey can see heat rays invisible to us. Some butterflies and bees can see ultraviolet light, also invisible to us, that flowers reflect.

The brimstone butterfly has special patterns on its wings to attract other butterflies that can see ultraviolet light.

# Illusions and Images

The brain has a big part to play in producing the images we see. It interprets nerve impulses from the eyes to create the image that we automatically see. But the brain can easily be fooled, especially if the eyes give it one message when it is expecting another. Tricks called optical illusions can deceive your brain into seeing something that's not there, but they help you understand how your vision really works.

## Blind spot

The optic nerve, which carries nerve impulses from the eye to the brain, joins the eye at a place near the middle of the retina. (You can see this in the diagram on page 14.) There are no light-detecting rods or cones at this spot at the back of the eye, and, for this reason, it is called the blind spot. You don't normally notice this gap in your vision because the brain cleverly "fills in" the missing information from the images surrounding the blind spot.

## TRY THIS

### Spots before your eyes

You will need a piece of cardboard that is about 5 inches (12 cm) square, along with a black marker or felt-tip pen. To find your blind spot, draw a cross "+" and a circle "o" on the card about 2 1/2 inches (6 cm) apart. Now hold up the card about 12 inches (30 cm) from your face. Cover your left eye and focus with your right eye on the cross. Slowly bring the card toward you. When the circle reaches the blind spot of your right eye, your brain will fill in the gap with just a blank card, and the circle will magically disappear.

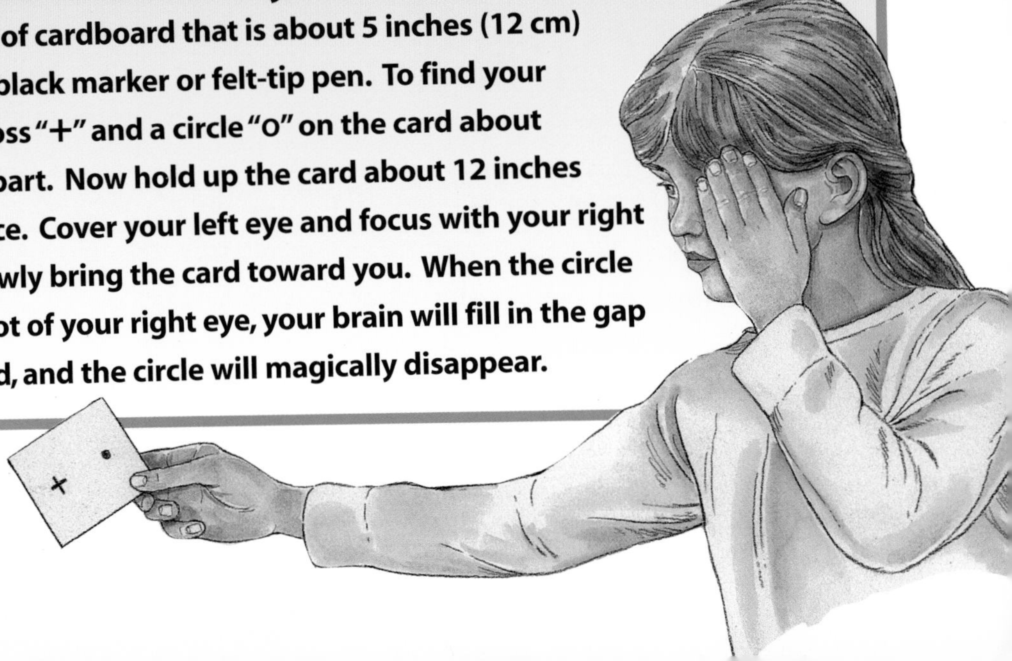

## Optical illusions

Try fooling your brain with the optical illusions here. You'll find that your brain makes all kinds of assumptions about what it can see, even when it's wrong!

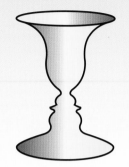

If you stare at this grid, you can see paler green small squares between the large squares, but they're not really there.

Look at this goblet. Can you see the two people who would drink from it?

Look at the two horizontal lines. Which one is longer? Now measure them to see if you are right.

## Did You Know?

A camera is like a human eye. It is a light-proof box with a lens at the front that focuses light on a film at the back of the camera. A diaphragm (like the iris in the eye) opens and closes a hole (like the pupil) to control the amount of light entering the camera. A shutter opens just long enough to let in enough light to take the picture. The photographer focuses the lens by moving it in and out (unlike the lens in the eye, which focuses by changing its thickness). As in the eye, the image on the film is upside-down, but we can easily solve that by turning our photos right-side up!

*Mirror*

*The light's path to the eye*

*Lens*

## Amazing Fact

If we watch a series of images in rapid succession, there is a slight delay before one image fades in the brain and is replaced by the next one. This is called persistence of vision, and it's crucial to how movies and television work. The movements we see on screen are really an illusion. We actually see twenty-four to thirty stationary images per second, but our brain "hangs on" to one image before receiving the next, so it looks like continuous movement.

**17**

# Good Vibrations

**Just like light, sound is a kind of energy – energy you can hear rather than see. Sound travels through the air as a series of vibrations called sound waves. It can also travel through liquids and solids. Unlike light, sound can't travel millions of miles across empty space. It must have air, water, or another substance to move through as a vibration.**

## Noise or notes?

Sound energy is made when something vibrates, making the air around it vibrate, too. For example, when you pluck a guitar string or bang a drum, it vibrates. The vibrations pass into the air and travel to your ears. You can see a guitar string vibrate, but you can't always see sound vibrations – for example, hand clapping.

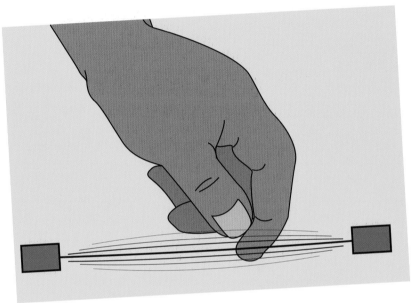

Hand clapping or banging two stones together makes a sound that scientists call "noise." Noise doesn't have any particular musical note, or pitch. Musical instruments produce sounds that do have pitch. You can hear the separate notes.

## Amazing Fact

Doctors are using sound to help broken bones heal faster. Directing sound waves at broken bones makes them form new bone at a faster rate. This technique is called Sonic Accelerated Fracture Healing.

## TRY THIS

### Wineglass whine

You can amaze your friends by making a glass "sing" with this trick. Take an empty wineglass and hold the base firmly on a tabletop. Lick one finger and rub it round and round the rim of the glass. It takes a little practice, but soon the glass will "sing" with a pure, high note.

## Detecting sound waves

Sound waves travel through the air as vibrations. You can prove this by making your own sound detector. Get a glass bowl, a piece of plastic wrap, a rubber band, and some salt or sugar. Stretch the plastic wrap tight across the top of the bowl. Use the rubber band to hold it in place. Sprinkle a few grains of salt or sugar on the middle of the plastic wrap. Now make a loud sound nearby by clapping your hands together. The sound vibrations in the air make the plastic wrap vibrate, causing the salt crystals to jump up and down. This shows that sound vibrations are made when you clap your hands, even though you can't actually see them.

## Making music

Instruments make musical sounds in three main ways. Stringed instruments have vibrating strings. These may be bowed to make them vibrate (as in a violin), plucked (as in a harp or guitar), or struck (as in a piano). In wind instruments, a vibrating column of air inside the instrument produces sound. The air is set in motion by a reed vibrating (as in an oboe or clarinet) or by the player's lips vibrating (as in a bugle or trumpet). We all know that hitting something to make it vibrate produces sounds. You can make music by hitting the metal of a triangle or cymbals or the strips of wood in a xylophone, or by banging on a drum (although your parents might not call it music).

Although supersonic jet planes are very noisy, you can't hear one coming towards you because it flies faster than the speed of sound, so it passes you before its sound arrives. When the sound does reach your ears, it is in the form of a shock wave that you hear as a loud bang – known as a sonic boom.

# Speedy Sound

**Sound isn't as fast as light, but it's still fast. Sound waves travel through dry air at a speed of 1,126 feet (343 m) per second when the temperature is 68°F (20°C). They go even faster through denser substances. In seawater, they move at around 5,000 feet (1,500 m) per second, and in iron and steel at an amazing 16,000 feet (5,000 m) per second – which is faster than a high-speed bullet.**

## Sound signals

Workers in tunnels and prisoners in jails make use of the fact that sound travels well in solids. They send signals to each other by tapping on metal pipes that run through the tunnel or prison. Hadrian's Wall, built in Scotland long ago by the ancient Romans, has clay pipes running along its length, and some historians think that bored Roman soldiers patrolling the wall used to tap messages to each other. Modern water engineers use the fact that sound vibrations travel well through metal by placing their ear at one end of a metal "listening stick," with the other end on the ground, to listen for water leaking out of underground pipes. Animals such as whales and dolphins make underwater cries that travel many miles (kilometers) at high speed, because sound travels much faster in water than in air.

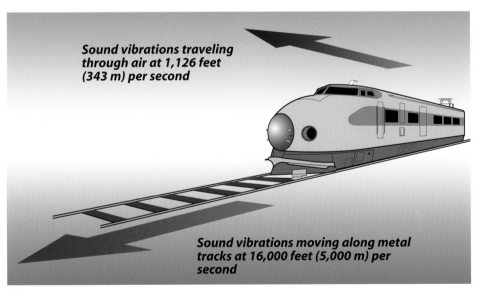

*Sound vibrations traveling through air at 1,126 feet (343 m) per second*

*Sound vibrations moving along metal tracks at 16,000 feet (5,000 m) per second*

**If you stand near a railroad line, you can hear the rumble of an approaching train vibrating the rails long before you can hear the train itself.**

## Sound science

One of the first relatively accurate measurements of the speed of sound was made by English scientist William Derham (1657–1735) in the early eighteenth century. Derham climbed to the top of a church tower, taking a stopwatch with him. A helper fired a cannon on a hilltop about 12 miles (20 km) away. Derham started his watch when he saw the flash of the cannon, and stopped it when he heard the bang. He now knew how long sound took to travel 12 miles, and from that he figured out the speed of sound. He calculated it to be 1,142 feet (348.1 m) per second, pretty close to modern measurements.

## Make a string telephone

You will need two empty tin cans or yogurt containers, a length of string, a nail, and a hammer. Use the nail and hammer to make a hole in the center of the base of each can. Thread the string through the hole in one can and knot it on the inside. Thread the other end of the string through the hole in the other can and knot it. Now get a friend to hold one can while you hold the other. Stretch the string tight and take turns speaking into the can. The speaker should keep the can close to his or her mouth, and the listener should cup the can over one ear. As long as you keep the string tight, the sound vibrations will travel along it and be easy to hear.

## Amazing Fact

Sound travels faster near the ground than up in the sky. As you go higher, the air gets colder and sound travels through it more slowly. Outside an aircraft flying at more than 32,000 feet (10,000 m) above the ground, the air temperature can be as low as -76°F (-60°C). Here, the speed of sound is about 965 feet (294 m) per second.

Another scientist who did early experiments with sound was the Irishman Robert Boyle. Around 1660, he took a glass bell jar and put it over a ticking watch. With the jar in place, he could still hear the watch. He then connected a vacuum pump to the jar and pumped the air out. As the air was removed, the sound of the watch got fainter and fainter until, with all the air pumped out, the watch was silent. It hadn't stopped, though. The second hand was still moving. This showed that sound does not travel in a vacuum.

**Robert Boyle (1627–1691), an Irish chemist and physicist**

# How Loud?

**Sounds don't just come in different notes. They come in different volumes as well – from the tiniest whisper to a fire engine's siren that's so loud it hurts. The loudness of a sound depends on how big the vibrations are. Quiet sounds are small vibrations that carry only a little bit of sound energy through the air. Loud sounds are big vibrations carrying large amounts of energy. The more energy that is carried in the vibrations, the louder the sound will be.**

## Noise numbers

Loudness is measured in units called decibels, which are named after the American inventor of the telephone, Alexander Graham Bell (1847-1922).

What's the quietest sound you can hear? A ticking watch? Leaves rustling gently in the breeze? Quiet sounds like these measure about 10 to 20 on the decibel scale, which is as low as most people can hear. Some large-eared animals that are active during the night can hear sounds that are even quieter. A barn owl can detect the tread of a mouse on the floor of a barn!

The loudest sounds of all include big explosions and the sound of a space rocket taking off. These may exceed 150dB (decibels). Very loud sounds can be painful and damage your hearing. That's why you automatically put your hands over your ears if a car or fire alarm goes off nearby. Listening to loud sounds for too long – like a personal stereo with the volume turned up too high – can damage your hearing. That's why people who work with or near loud noises, such as airport workers and road repairmen, wear ear protectors to muffle the sound and protect their ears.

## Louder and louder

Sounds can be made louder, or amplified, using electronic equipment. That's how bands make their music loud enough for everyone to hear at a concert. A microphone picks up the sound and converts it into a series of electrical signals. An amplifier adds electric energy to make the signals bigger, and a loudspeaker converts the signals back into sounds.

**Earphones are small loudspeakers.**

## Make vibrations

You can experiment with the loudness of sound by making a simple box guitar. You will need an open-topped cardboard box (an empty tissue box or shoe box with the top removed is fine) and a long rubber band. Stretch the rubber band around the box. Now "twang" the rubber band with your finger. Try twanging it gently and then twang it harder. Can you hear a difference? The loudness of the sound that you produce depends on how hard you pluck the rubber band and how big the sound vibrations are.

## Amazing Fact

The loudest sound ever heard on Earth by humans was probably the volcanic explosion that blew most of the Indonesian island of Krakatoa to bits at around 10 a.m. on August 27, 1883. It was heard by people up to 3,000 miles (5,000 km) away.

## Did You Know?

A watch ticking is about 10dB on the decibel scale.

Each time 10 decibels are added on the decibel scale, the loudness is multiplied 10 times. So a 40dB sound is 10 times as loud as a 30dB sound. Here are some typical examples of loudness on the decibel scale.

The sound of a car engine is about 80dB.

A birdsong is about 25dB.

# High or Low?

**The highness or lowness of a sound is known as its pitch. For example, the sound of a whistle is high-pitched, while a bass guitar makes a low-pitched sound. Some animals can hear sounds of a much higher or lower pitch than human beings. Just like volume, pitch has to do with sound vibrations.**

## Who can hear what?

The pitch of a sound depends on the number of vibrations produced per second, which is called the sound's frequency.

Pitch is measured in units called hertz, where 1 hertz (1 Hz) equals one vibration per second. A frequency of 1 Hz would be an extremely low sound, and human hearing is best at a much higher frequency of about 1,000 Hz. Our hearing gets worse as we get older. Children are much better at hearing than adults. You can hear sounds from about 20 to 20,000 Hz, but your parents or grandparents may not be able to hear

very high-pitched sounds well. That's why they are always asking you to speak up.

Some animals can hear sounds that are too low in pitch for us to hear. Other animals can hear sounds well above the top of the human hearing range. Bats and dolphins can hear sounds with a pitch as high as a whopping 120,000 Hz or even higher. Many insects also produce very high-pitched sounds. So what seems to us to be a silent night might really be alive with squeaks and chirrups. We just don't have the right sort of ears to hear them.

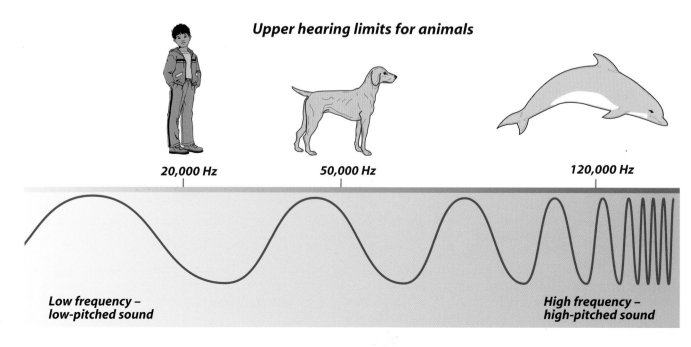

***Upper hearing limits for animals***

*20,000 Hz*    *50,000 Hz*    *120,000 Hz*

*Low frequency –*
*low-pitched sound*

*High frequency –*
*high-pitched sound*

## Bottle band

Find four or five similar empty glass bottles and put different amounts of water in each. If you blow across the top of the bottle, you will vibrate the column of air inside the bottle and make it produce a sound. The bottle with the most water – and therefore the shortest air column – will produce the highest pitch. Many wind instruments produce musical notes of different pitch by varying the length of the vibrating column of air inside them.

You may have noticed that the sound of a siren on a police car or ambulance seems to stay steady as it comes toward you. But as it goes past, the pitch of the siren falls. This is called the Doppler effect, named after the Austrian scientist Christian Doppler (1803–1853), who was the first to explain it, in 1842. As the car approaches, the sound waves coming toward you from the siren are bunched slightly together because the car is moving with the sound waves. If the waves are closer together, they have a higher frequency and form a constant high pitch. As the car moves away from you, the sound waves are stretched farther apart, the frequency drops, and the pitch of the sound seems to fall.

## Changing pitch

Make a simple box guitar using a box and a rubber band, as on page 23, but this time, add some more rubber bands of different thicknesses. You should find that thicker bands produce lower notes. You can also make the note higher by stretching the rubber band tighter. If you look at a stringed instrument such as a guitar, you'll see that it uses strings of different thickness, some stretched tighter than others, to make different notes.

# All Ears

**Everyone knows what ears are. They're those things on the sides of your head that hold your sunglasses up. Wrong! Those are just the outside part of your ears. In fact, ears are made up of three parts called the outer, middle, and inner ear, and they reach right inside your head to your brain. It's your brain that actually "hears" sounds, by translating the signals your ears send to it.**

## How you hear

Ears work by detecting the vibrations that sounds make in the air. The outer ear – which scientists call the pinna – is the part you can see. It is funnel-shaped to catch sounds and send them down a tunnel inside your head that is about 1 inch (2–3 cm) long. This tunnel is called the ear canal. At the end of the ear canal, the vibrations hit your eardrum – a tightly stretched piece of skin similar to the skin of a real drum. The vibrations in the air make the eardrum vibrate.

Behind the eardrum is an area called the middle ear, which contains three tiny bones. The first bone, the hammer, is joined to the eardrum. Its other end hinges with the anvil, which is in turn joined to the stirrup. When the eardrum vibrates, these three hinged bones pass on the vibrations to the inner ear. The middle ear is full of air. It is connected to your throat by the eustachian tube. Swallowing helps to make your ears feel better when there's a sudden change in air pressure, such as when your plane takes off. When you swallow, air passes up the tube to balance the pressure in your middle ear.

In the inner ear, the cochlea, a snail-shaped tube, picks up vibrations from the stirrup and turns them into electric signals. These signals travel along nerves to the brain, which then tells us if the telephone is ringing or if the dog is barking. Also attached to the cochlea are three loops, called semicircular canals, that tell the brain the position of the head and give us our sense of balance.

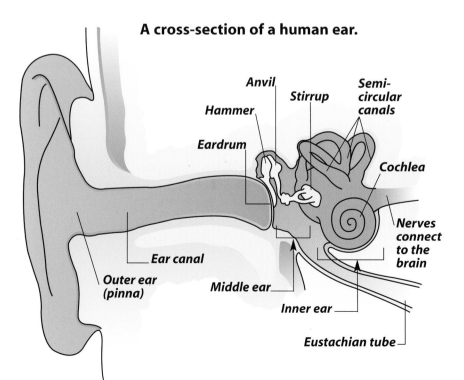

**A cross-section of a human ear.**

Anvil

Stirrup

Semi-circular canals

Hammer

Eardrum

Cochlea

Nerves connect to the brain

Ear canal

Outer ear (pinna)

Middle ear

Inner ear

Eustachian tube

# Did You Know?

While some animals don't have ears (such as sharks and snakes), most animals depend on their hearing for hunting down food, listening for anything that might be creeping up behind them, and communicating with friends and family. This African serval hunts in the dark. It swivels its ears around to face the direction a sound is coming from so that it can track down prey and pounce with deadly accuracy.

## Amazing Fact

Spiders lack ears like ours, but they can "hear" with special sensors – called slit sense organs – that detect vibrations on their exoskeleton (the hard outer "skin" of insects and similar creatures). Spiders can also pick up vibrations through the air and ground using tiny hairs on their legs and body. These hairs pick up air movements and buzzing sounds of insects flying up to 12 inches (30 cm) away.

## TRY THIS

### The sound of yourself

When you hear yourself speaking, most of the sound gets to your ears by passing through the bones of your skull. To find out what you really sound like to other people, get somebody to make a tape recording of you speaking. When it's played back, you'll be amazed how different you sound.

## TRY THIS

### Surround sound

Everybody has two ears. Unless a sound comes from directly in front or directly behind us, it arrives at one ear a fraction of a second before it reaches the other. The tiny delay enables our brain to figure out where a sound is coming from. To test this, have a friend sit blindfolded in a chair. Get other people to sit or stand around and make noises. See how well your friend can tell where each sound is coming from. Now try the test on other people. Are some more accurate than others?

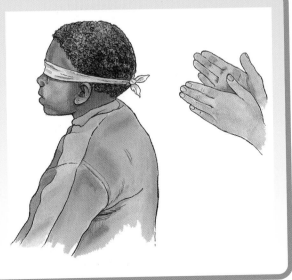

# Echo Effects

Like light, sound can bounce! It can reflect off hard surfaces such as cliffs, buildings, or the walls in an empty room, just like light reflects off a mirror. A reflected sound is called an echo. Since we know the speed of sound, we can use a method called echo sounding to find out how far away an object is by measuring echoes. Some animals use this method to spot their enemies or find their prey in the dark.

Ships can use echo sounding to check the depth of the water. It's also used to measure distances to icebergs and groups of fish.

## Bouncing sound

If you stand in a pedestrian underpass and shout out loud, you'll frighten people. Apart from that, you'll also hear your shout repeated a second or two later. This is an echo, caused by the sound waves reflecting off the walls of the underpass. You can also hear echoes in the countryside if you shout at a cliff or cave wall.

Because we know the speed of sound, echoes can be used to calculate the distance to an object. Such "echo sounding" works best with high-pitched sounds that have a frequency of more than 20,000 Hz. These sounds are called ultrasound because they're too high for humans to hear. A special receiver picks up the sounds after they bounce off objects.

Echo sounding (sometimes called sonar) is used by ships and by submarines for measuring distances underwater – such as how deep the sea is. A ship has an ultrasound transmitter and receiver mounted on its hull. The transmitter sends out a series of ultrasound signals. They travel through the water, bounce off the seabed, and go back to the ship, where the receiver picks them up. How long the ultrasound takes to reach the seabed and bounce back to the ship tells sailors the depth of the water.

Some kinds of bats use ultrasound to find their insect prey in the dark. They send out a series of ultrasonic squeaks and detect any echoes that bounce off insects flying nearby. They quickly close in on their prey and use their wings to scoop it toward their mouth.

Ultrasound also has medical uses. It can be used to scan a person's body. Some body parts, such as bone, reflect ultrasound better than others, so an ultrasound scan can make a picture of different tissues in the body.

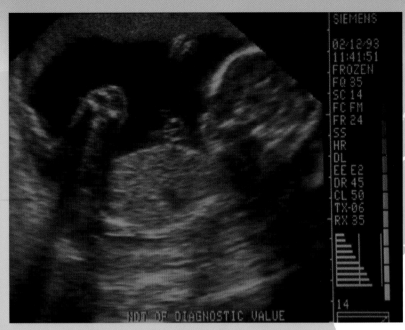

SIEMENS
02/12/93
11:41:51
FROZEN
FQ 35
SC 14
FC FM
FR 24
SS
HR
DL
EE E2
DR 45
CL 50
TX-06
RX 35

14

NOT OF DIAGNOSTIC VALUE

This is an ultrasound image of an unborn baby in its mother's womb.

### Making waves

You can imitate sound waves by using ripples on the surface of water. You will need a large bowl, water, a small stone, and a hard object such as a strip of metal. Put about 1 inch (2–3 cm) of water in the bottom of the bowl. Drop the stone in the middle, and watch how the circular waves ripple outward. Then stand the metal strip in the bowl. Now, when you drop in the stone, the strip reflects the ripples, just like waves of ultrasound in a sonar echo.

Dolphins use ultrasound waves to probe the world around them and to communicate with other dolphins. These waves are too high for humans to hear, but they can pass through a yard (meter) of mud and tell dolphins the difference between solid and hollow objects, such as between rocks and fish.

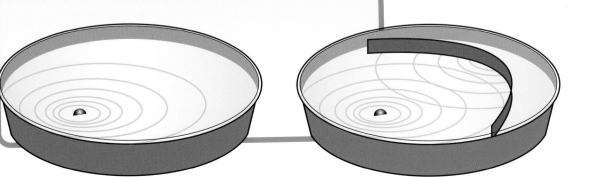

# Making Waves

**As you know, light and sound are both forms of energy. They have something else in common as well. They both travel as waves, but we can't see them like other familiar kinds of waves, such as ripples on a pond, after you throw in a stone, or waves of seawater, rolling onto a beach.**

## What are waves?

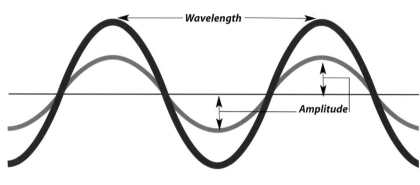

A wave happens when something moves up and down. These regular up-and-down movements can carry energy from one place to another. All waves have a series of peaks and troughs, which look like a row of hills and valleys. The distance between any two neighboring peaks (or troughs) is called the wavelength. Waves whose wavelength is short have a high frequency, which means a lot of waves pass in one second. Light has an extremely short wavelength and travels at a mind-boggling 186,000 miles (300,000 km) per second. Nothing travels faster.

The strength of a wave is measured by its amplitude, which is the height of the wave above its average position. The amplitude lets you know how much energy the wave is carrying, so light waves with a large amplitude are very bright. Sound waves with a high amplitude are very loud.

## Amazing Fact

**The largest sea waves, called tsunamis, are caused by earthquakes, landslides, and volcanic eruptions on the seabed. The tallest known tsunami, reaching a height of 1,700 feet (520 m), occurred in Lituya Bay, Alaska, in 1958.**

## Wave movement

**When a wave moves through a material – such as a sound wave traveling through air – the material itself does not move along with the wave. You can see this with waves on water. You'll need a cork, some pebbles, and a pond. Throw the cork into the pond. Next throw a pebble near the floating cork. As the waves, or ripples, travel past the cork, the cork just bobs up and down. It does not travel along with the ripples.**

# Glossary

**amplitude**
The height of a wave above its average position

**concave**
Curving inward

**convex**
Curving outward

**decibel**
A unit of measurement of sound loudness

**echo**
A sound heard for a second time after it bounces off a distant object

**eclipse**
What happens when one object in space passes in front of another and blocks out its light. In a solar eclipse, the Moon blocks out the Sun.

**frequency**
For any wave motion, the number of vibrations that occur in one second

**lens**
A piece of curved and polished glass or plastic, used to bend (refract) light

**light**
A type of energy that we can see, produced mainly by very hot objects such as the Sun or the filament of an electric lightbulb

**opaque**
Describing a material that will not let light pass through it

**pitch**
In sound, the highness or lowness of a note, measured by the sound's frequency

**prism**
A triangular block of glass or other transparent material that can split white light into a spectrum

**reflection**
The change in the direction of light when it bounces off a mirror

**refraction**
The change in the direction of light when it passes from one transparent material into another

**rods and cones**
Special cells in the human eye that detect light. Cone cells are sensitive to color, but rod cells are not.

**shadow**
An area where light rays are blocked from entering by something opaque

**sonar**
A way of detecting objects underwater by bouncing sound waves off them

**sound**
A type of energy produced by vibrating objects. It takes the form of waves in air or another material.

**spectrum**
A range of colors, including the colors of the rainbow, produced when a prism splits up white light

**transparent**
Describing a material that lets light pass through it

**tsunami**
An enormous sea wave caused by an earthquake, a landslide, or a volcanic eruption

**ultrasound**
Sound waves whose frequency is higher than humans can hear

**vibration**
Rapid up-and-down or side-to-side movements of an object, such as the head of a drum or the string of a guitar that is being played

**wave**
A regularly repeating motion, in a medium (such as air or water) or in space, that carries energy

**wavelength**
For any wave motion, the distance between any two neighboring crests or troughs

# Index